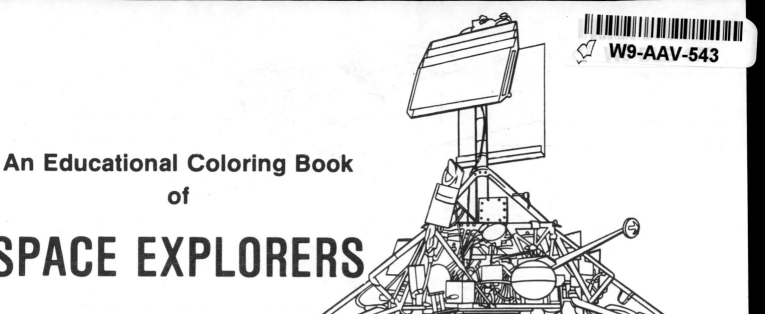

An Educational Coloring Book of

SPACE EXPLORERS

EDITOR
Linda Spizzirri

COPY REFERENCE
Museums of Science
and Industry

ILLUSTRATION
Peter M. Spizzirri

COVER ART
Peter M. Spizzirri

CONTENTS

An Educational Coloring Book of SPACE EXPLORERS • Published by SPIZZIRRI PUBLISHING CO., INC., P.O. BOX 664 MEDINAH, ILLINOIS 60157. No part of this publication may be reproduced by any means without the express written consent of the publisher. All national and international rights reserved on the entire contents of this publication.
Printed in U.S.A.

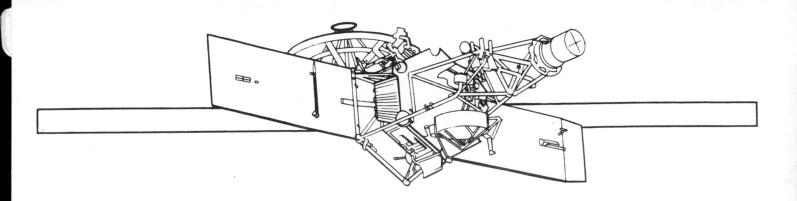

NAME:

INTERESTING FACTS:

GODDARD ROCKETS

Robert H. Goddard designed the world's first liquid propellant rockets. The first one (illustrated), built in 1926, flew to an altitude of 41 feet in 2½ seconds. Goddard built his final rocket in 1941. The 1941 rocket incorporates many design elements of today's larger rockets. The 1926 and 1941 rockets represent the beginning and the end of Goddard's efforts to develop high altitude liquid propellant rockets.

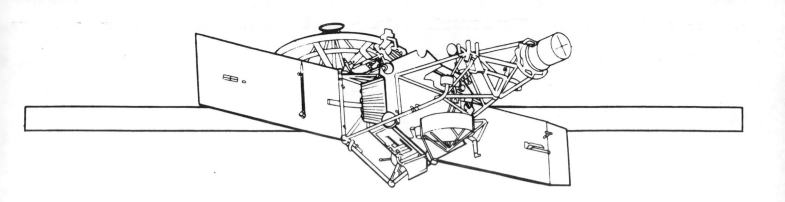

NAME:	SPUTNIK I AND EXPLORER I (First Earth Satellites)
INTERESTING FACTS:	Sputnik I was the first USSR satellite, and Explorer I was the first United States satellite, to orbit the Earth. Sputnik I was orbited on October 4, 1957 and operated for 22 days. Sputnik transmitted internal and external temperature information and provided important orbital data concerning atmospheric and electron densities at high altitudes. The United States orbited Explorer I, January 31, 1958 and it operated for 105 days. Explorer I transmitted data on micrometeoroids, cosmic radiation and internal and external temperatures. The satellite's data led to the discovery of the Van Allen Radiation Belts.

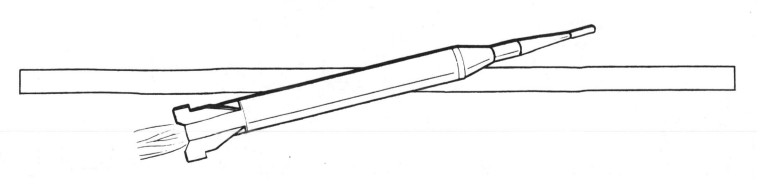

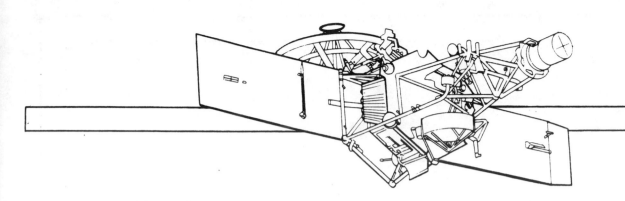

ROCKET **A**:   JANUARY, 1958

NAME: JUPITER "C"

INTERESTING FACTS: On first attempt, this rocket successfully launched the free world's first satellite, "Explorer I".

ROCKET **B**:   MARCH, 1959

NAME: JUNO II

INTERESTING FACTS: The Juno II rocket launched the first free world solar satellite named, "Pioneer IV." "Pioneer IV" has the distinction of being the first U.S. payload projected to permanent escape from Earth.

ROCKET **C**:   MAY, 1959

NAME: JUPITER

INTERESTING FACTS: Jupiter successfully launched the first space shot that accomplished the return to Earth of the two primates Able and Baker.

ROCKET **D**:   May, 1961

NAME: REDSTONE

INTERESTING FACTS: The United State's first manned space flight, project Mercury capsule, was launched and boosted into space by this rocket.

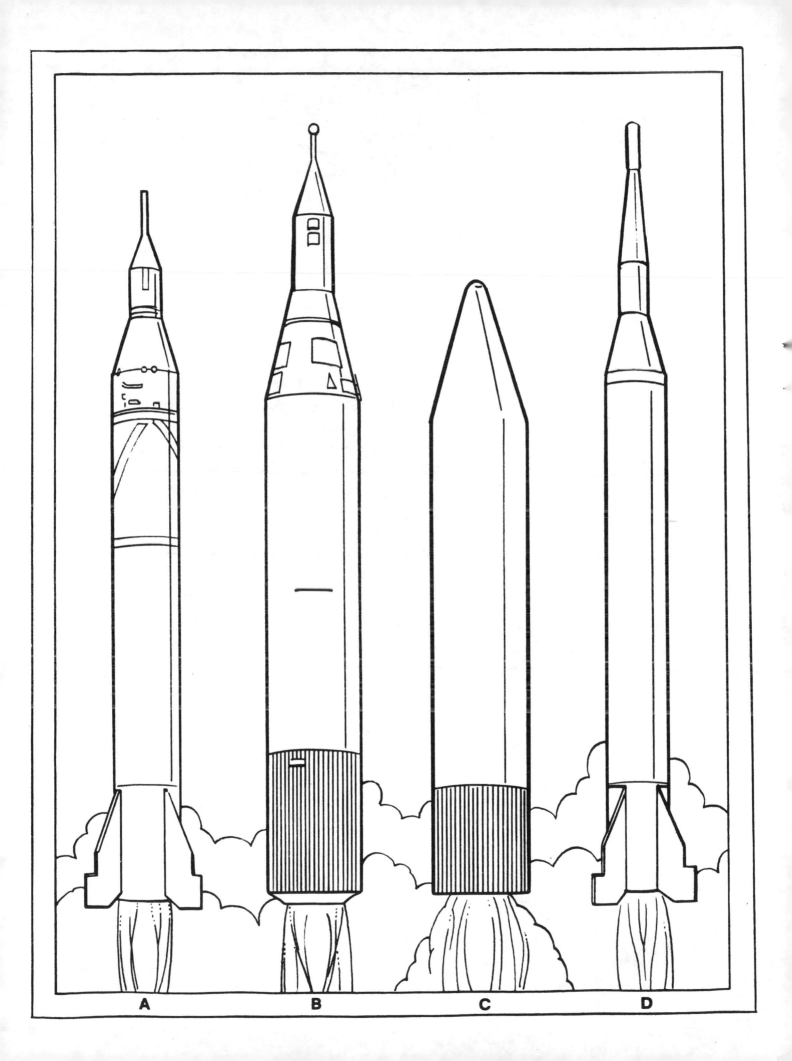

A   B   C   D

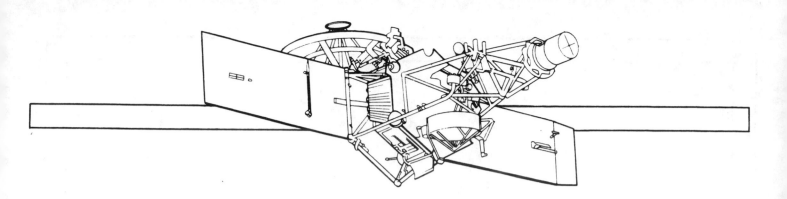

NAME:	RANGER
INTERESTING FACTS:	Launched by Atlas-Agena vehicles between 1961 and 1965, the Ranger spacecraft provided scientists with their first close look at the surface of the Moon. The Ranger's 65 hour journey ended in a crash on the surface of the Moon. During the final phases of the flight, the spacecraft transmitted many valuable pictures to Earth of the rapidly approaching lunar surface. These pictures revealed many details that could not be seen through telescopes on Earth.

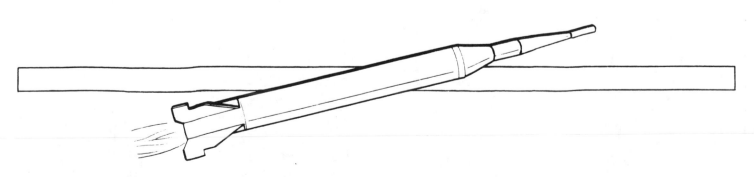

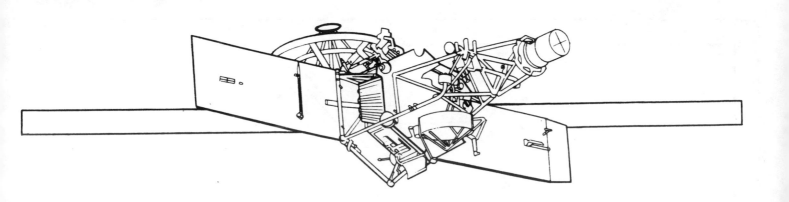

NAME: MARINER 2

INTERESTING FACTS: On December 14, 1962 Mariner 2 (M-2) flew to within 216 thousand miles of Venus and was 36 million miles from Earth. The 109 day flight was the first exploratory mission to another planet. Because of this mission we found that Venus is very hot, probably more than 800°F (427°C), and that there are no measurable magnetic fields or radiation belts. We lost contact with M-2 on January 2, 1963. It was last known to be in orbit around the sun.

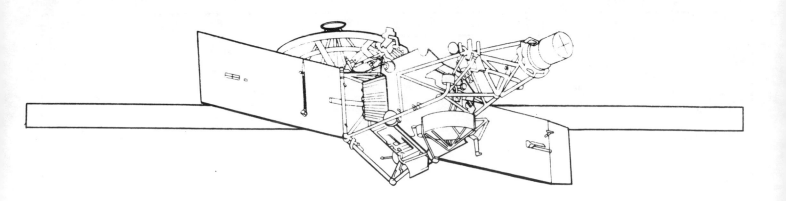

NAME:	SPACE WALK
INTERESTING FACTS:	On June 3, 1965 astronaut Major Edward H. White II, tethered by a golden cord, moved freely outside of his spacecraft, 100 miles above the Earth's surface. This historic date marked the longest walk in the deadly vacuum of space.

Although he was orbiting at 17,500 miles per hour, the astronaut had little sensation of speed and no sensation of falling. As astronaut White talked with the Gemini 4 command pilot, Major James A. McDivitt, through this 21 minute - 6,000 mile walk in space, the world was held in awe.

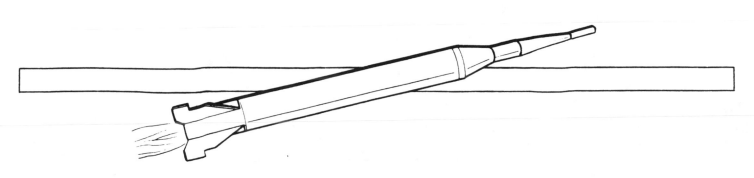

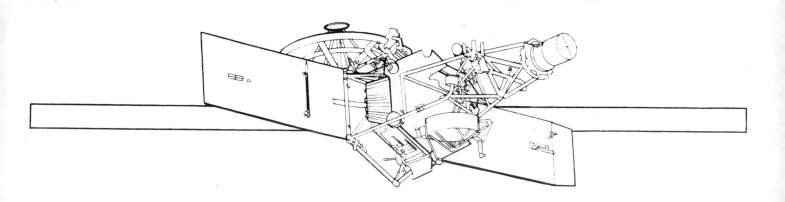

NAME:	MARINER IV

INTERESTING FACTS:

Mariner IV took its historic flight past Mars in 1965. Mariner IV transmitted to Earth the first photographs of the planet. The photographs, taken from 78,000 miles away, revealed eroded, meteorite-blasted craters. The pictures picked up craters with a diameter of 3 miles and many smaller features of the planet. This delighted the scientists, because 3 miles is something very small to pick up from a distance of 78,000 miles. Many scientists were surprised by the cratered surface of Mars.

In 1973 and 1974 Mariner space explorers gave us our first close-up look, via photographs, of the planets Venus and Mercury.

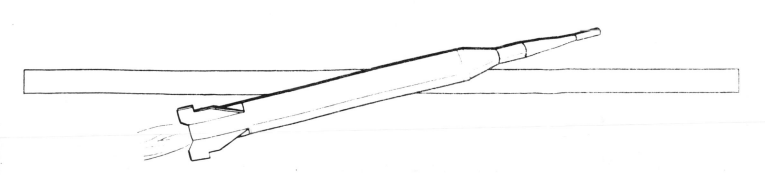

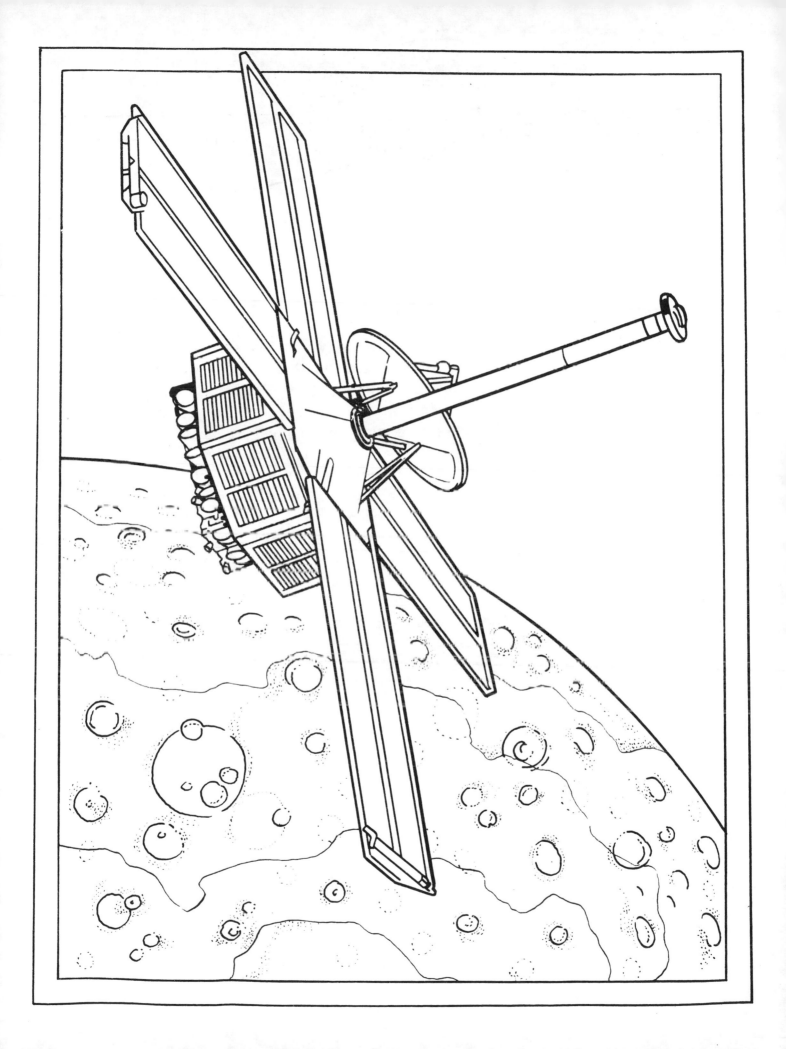

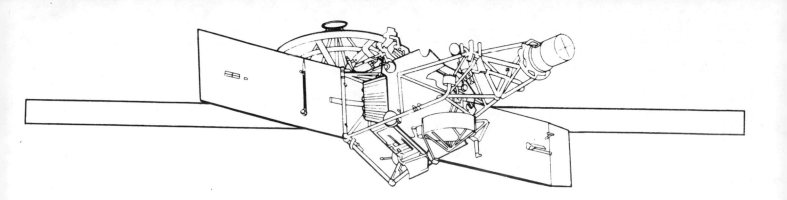

NAME: SURVEYOR

INTERESTING FACTS: Of the seven surveyors that were launched between 1966 and 1968, 5 made successful lunar landings. The Project Surveyor mission was to develop basic lunar soft-landing techniques, to survey for potential Apollo landing sites, and to obtain photos and other scientific information. The United States had set its sites on a manned lunar mission. The surveyor transmitted 87,632 pictures of the lunar surface, a small scoop at the end of an extended arm collected lunar soil samples and chemical analysis of the soil was performed.

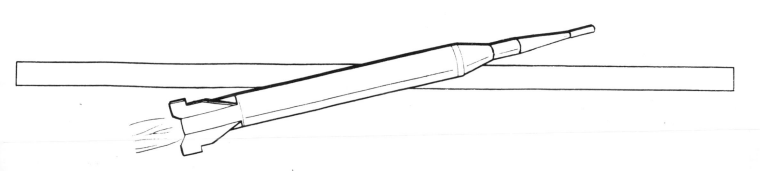

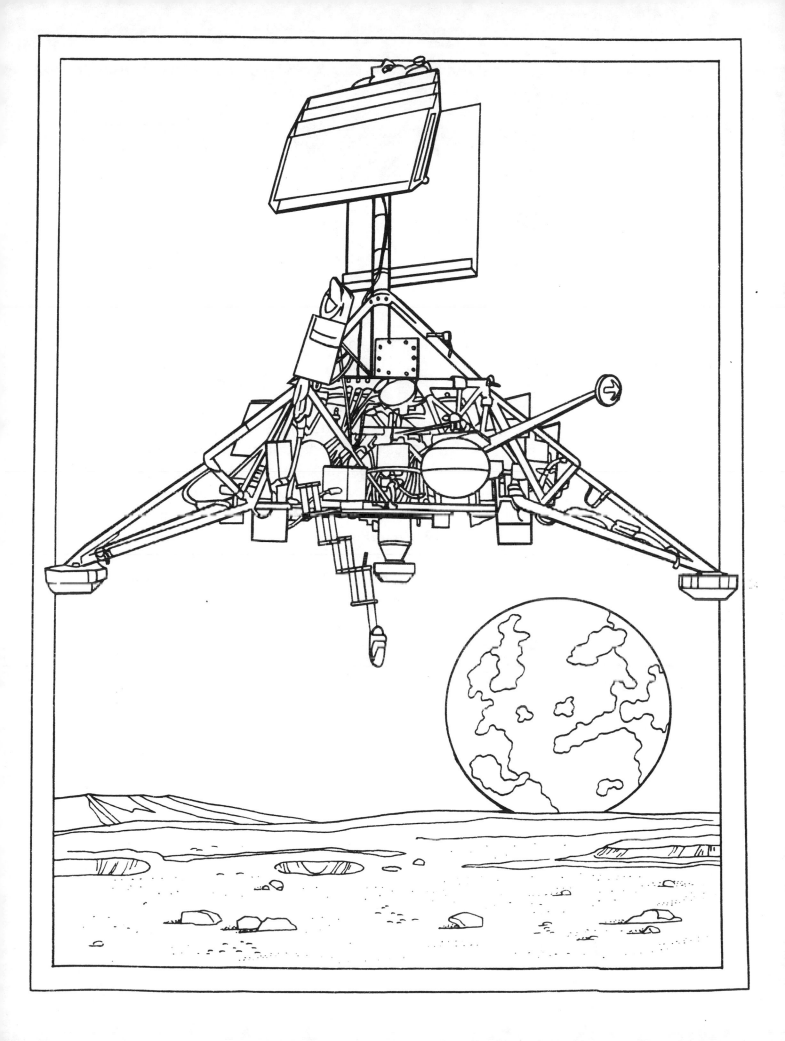

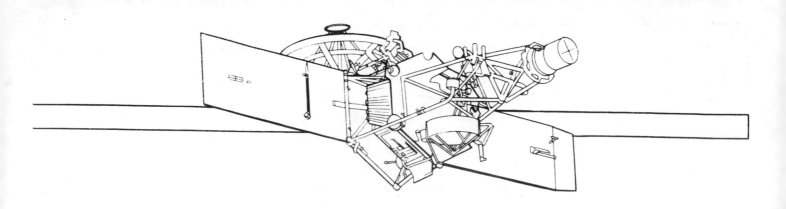

NAME:	SPACESUIT
MISSION:	APOLLO II
INTERESTING FACTS:	This spacesuit was worn by astronaut "Buzz" Aldrin during the historic Apollo II mission. During this mission on July 16-24, 1969, man took his first steps on the surface of the moon. The aluminum-coated suit was pressurized, insulating the astronaut, and included an oxygen supply and system for communication with the spacecraft. The Lunar Module is reflected in astronaut Aldrin's helmet visor.

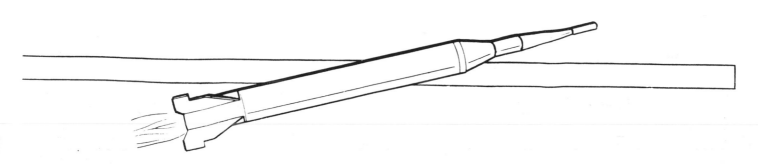

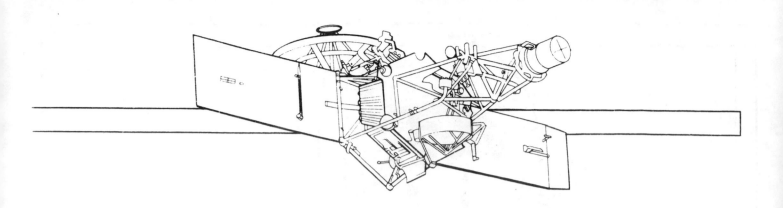

NAME:	LUNAR MODULE
MISSION:	APOLLO II
INTERESTING FACTS:	The Lunar Module descended to the moon's surface, carrying astronauts Neil Armstrong and Buzz Aldrin, for man's first Moon walk. The four-legged landing gear was left behind when the upper stage, containing crew quarters and scientific equipment, returned to the mother craft. Antenna and other probes can be seen on the upper stage.

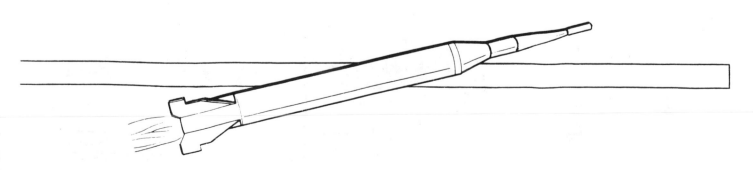

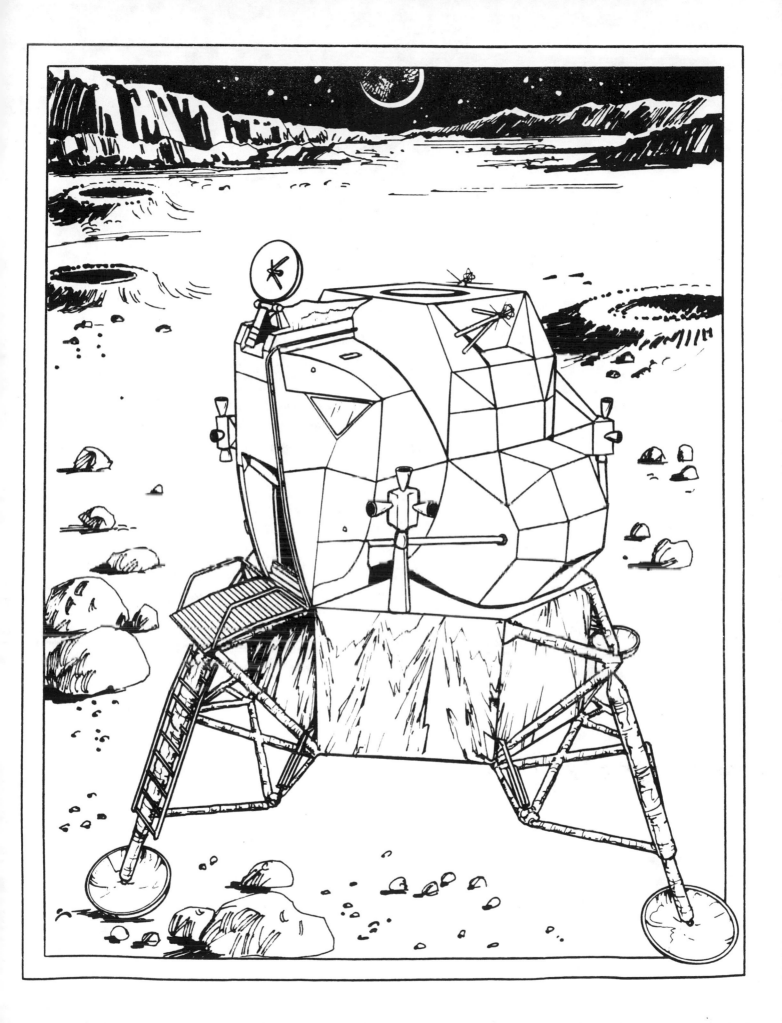

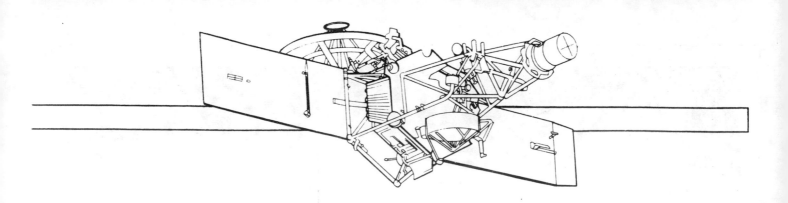

NAME:	SKYLAB ORBITAL WORKSHOP (OWS)
INTERESTING FACTS:	Skylab's 3-man crew lived and worked in the OWS for several months at a time, before the 48 foot, 78,000 pound Skylab was placed into orbit on May 14, 1973. Research projects included studying Earth resources and environments, observing solar processes, studying effects of long duration weightlessness on astronauts and experiments in material processing in the weightlessness and vacuum of space. Skylab was covered with a film of gold to protect it from the excessive solar heat. A Blue wing-like panel generated electric power from sunlight.

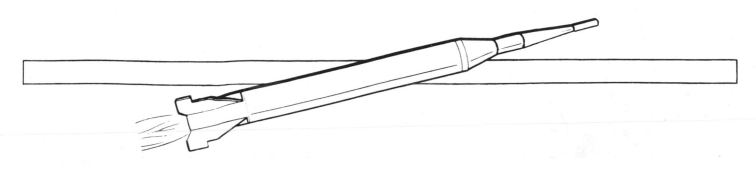

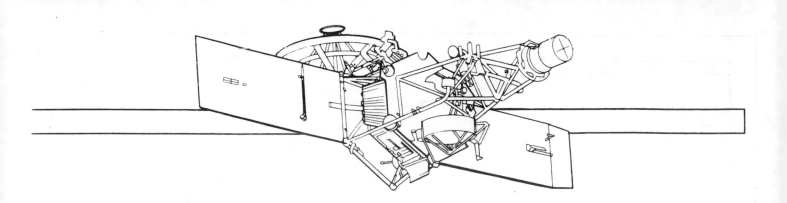

NAME: APOLLO-SOYUZ

INTERESTING FACTS: The Apollo-Soyuz Test Project (ASTP), was a joint program between United States and Russian scientists to develop and test a common docking system for spacecraft. In 1975 a successful mission was accomplished. It was a historic first time that the manned spacecraft of the two nations met in space.
On the left is the Apollo command and service module. In the center is the docking module. On the right is the Soyuz spacecraft including the spherical orbital module and the bell shaped descent module.

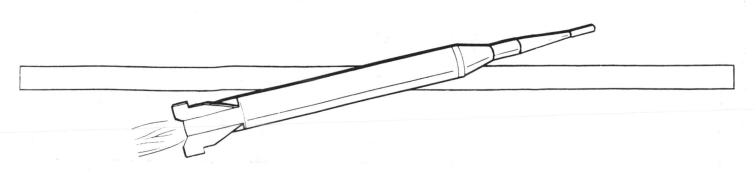

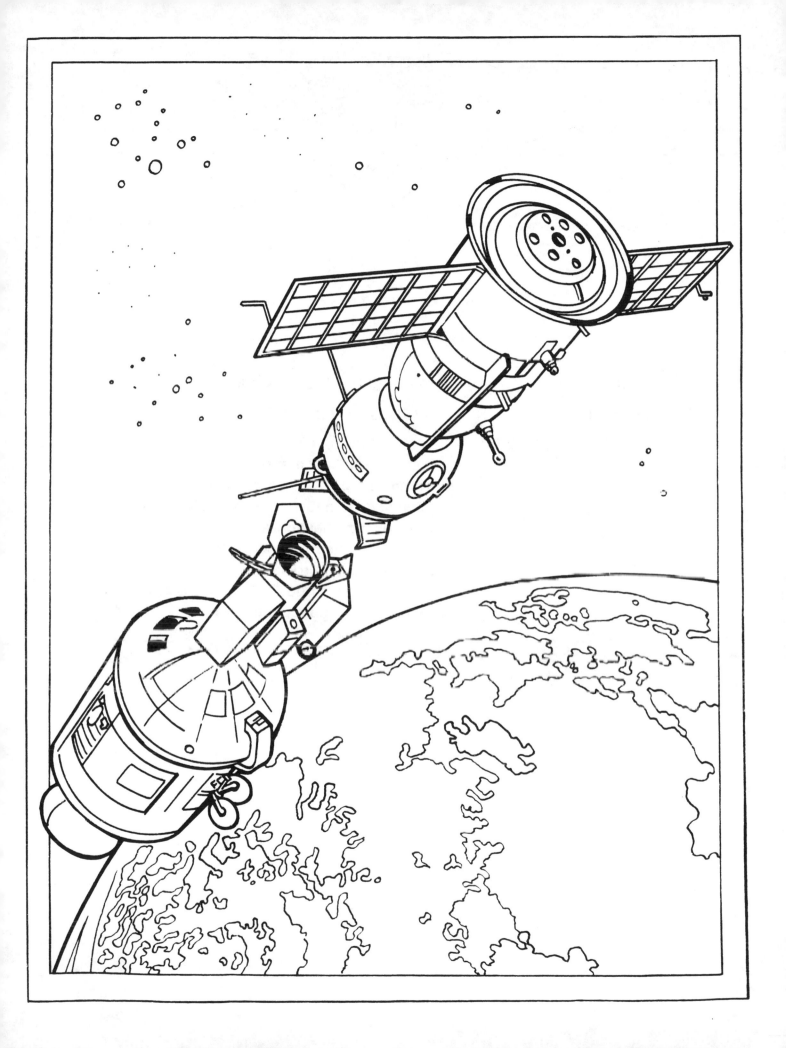

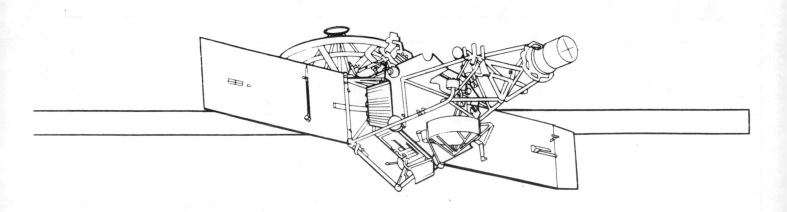

NAME:	APOLLO ROCKET ASSEMBLY
MISSION:	APOLLO-SOYUZ TEST PROJECT
INTERESTING FACTS:	The Apollo-Soyuz Test Project was the first international manned space flight, in which three U.S. astronauts and two Soviet cosmonauts docked their orbiting vehicles together and visited each other's spacecraft. The Apollo assembly consisted of a giant Saturn rocket, a launch vehicle, a service module jettisoned before reentry and a command module.

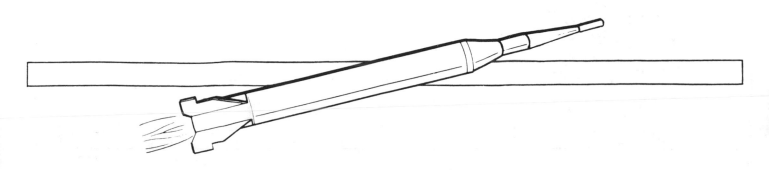

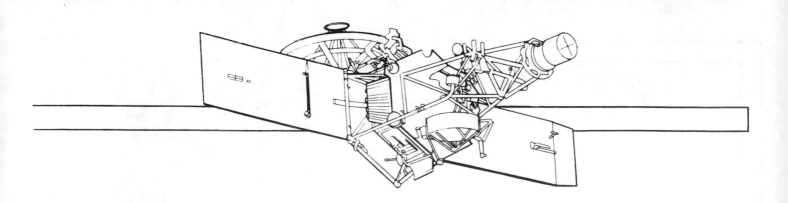

NAME: VOYAGER I

INTERESTING FACTS: Voyager I was launched on September 5, 1977. The purpose of its journey into space was to acquire new knowledge, information and photographs of the planet Jupiter, the largest planet in our solar system.

As Voyager I approached Jupiter in March of 1979 we started to receive photographs which gave very detailed information of the planet and its 4 known moons.

In November of 1980, Voyager I passed the planet Saturn and continued on its trajectory exiting our solar system and traveling into space never to return.

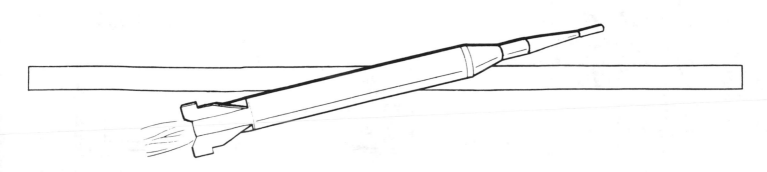

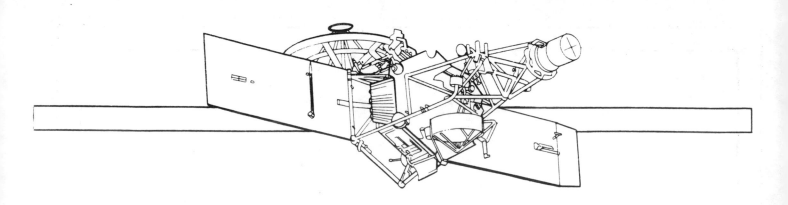

NAME: VOYAGER II

INTERESTING FACTS: Voyager II was launched 16 days ahead of Voyager I on August 20, 1977 and was on a slower trajectory. Voyager II was designed to back up and test the findings of Voyager I. The special mission of Voyager II is to investigate the outer planets of the solar system. Voyager II already passed the planet Jupiter in July of 1979. The scheduled course of the spacecraft includes a close look at the planet Saturn in August of 1981, Uranus in January of 1986 and Neptune in September of 1989. After completing the planetary missions and sending back detailed information and huge quantities of photographs, Voyager II like its sister ship Voyager I, will leave this solar system and travel to inter-stellar space, never to return.

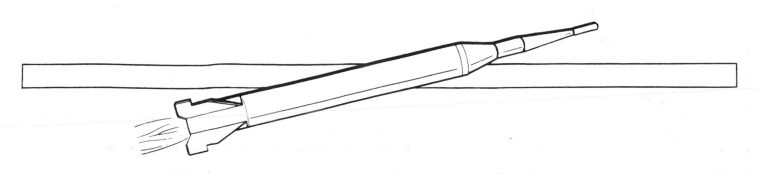

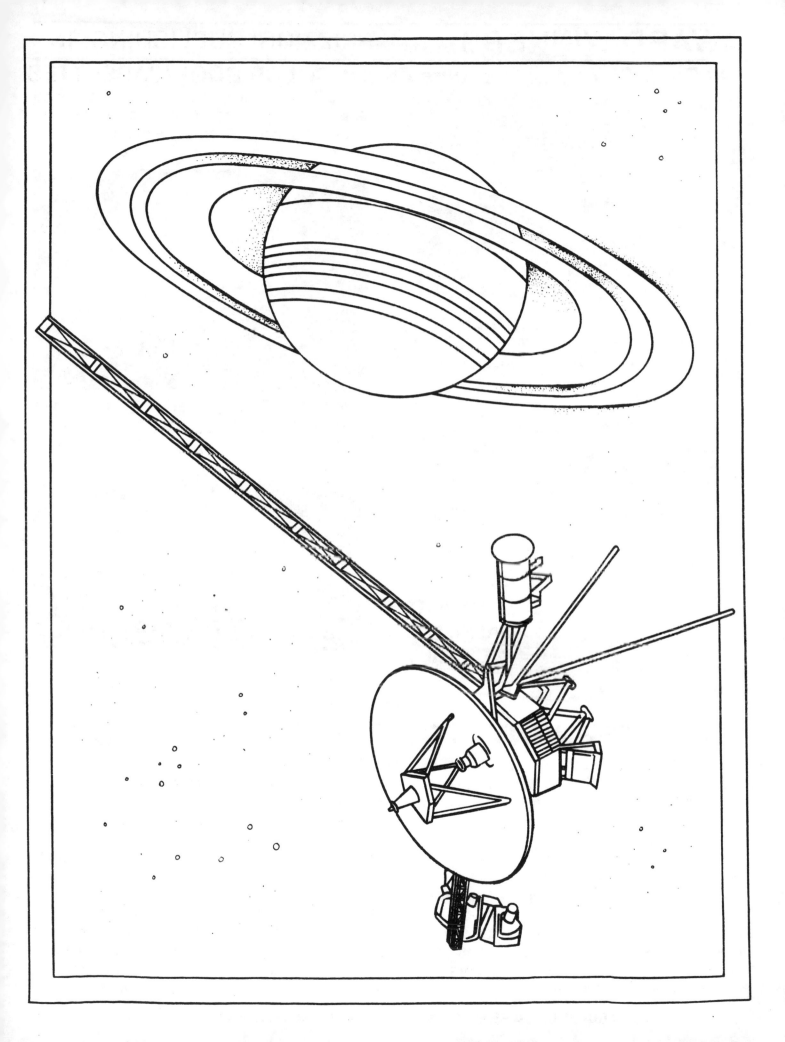

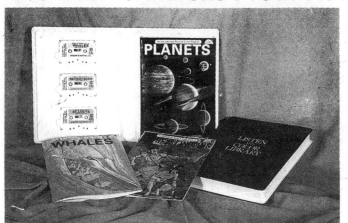

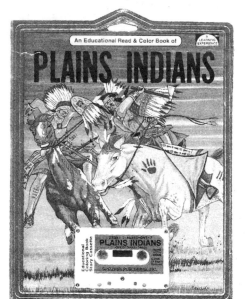